THE BEATLES
GREATEST HITS FOR HARMONICA

22 CLASSICS ARRANGED FOR C DIATONIC HARMONICA

Arranged by Eric J. Plahna

ISBN 978-0-88188-608-5

HAL•LEONARD®
CORPORATION
7777 W. BLUEMOUND RD. P.O. BOX 13819 MILWAUKEE, WI 53213

Visit Hal Leonard Online at
www.halleonard.com

HARMONICA NOTATION LEGEND

Harmonica music can be notated two different ways: on a *musical staff*, and in *tablature*.

THE MUSICAL STAFF shows pitches and rhythms and is divided by bar lines into measures. Pitches are named after the first seven letters of the alphabet.

TABLATURE graphically represents the harmonica music. Each note will be accompanied by a number, 1 through 10, indicating what hole you are to play. The arrow that follows indicates whether to blow or draw. (All examples are shown using a C diatonic harmonica.)

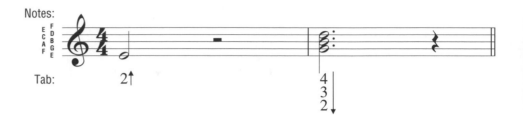

Blow (exhale) into 2nd hole.

Draw (inhale) 2nd, 3rd, & 4th holes together.

Notes on the C Harmonica

Exhaled (Blown) Notes

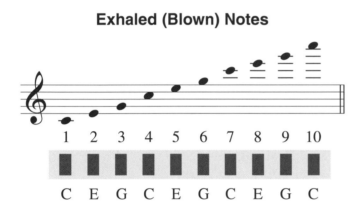

1	2	3	4	5	6	7	8	9	10
C	E	G	C	E	G	C	E	G	C

Inhaled (Drawn) Notes

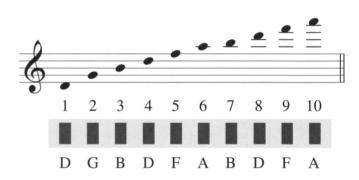

1	2	3	4	5	6	7	8	9	10
D	G	B	D	F	A	B	D	F	A

Bends

Blow Bends

- 1/4 step
- 1/2 step
- 1 step
- 1 1/2 steps

Draw Bends

- 1/4 step
- 1/2 step
- 1 step
- 1 1/2 steps

Definitions for Special Harmonica Notation

SLURRED BEND: Play (draw) 3rd hole, then bend the note down one whole step.

GRACE NOTE BEND: Starting with a pre-bent note, immediately release bend to the target note.

VIBRATO: Begin adding vibrato to the sustained note on beat 3.

TONGUE BLOCKING: Using your tongue to block holes 2 & 3, play octaves on holes 1 & 4.

NOTE: Tablature numbers in parentheses are used when:
- The note is sustained, but a new articulation begins (such as vibrato), or
- The quantity of notes being sustained changes, or
- A change in dynamics (volume) occurs.

Additional Musical Definitions

D.S. al Coda
- Go back to the sign (𝄋), then play until the measure marked "***To Coda,***" then skip to the section labelled "**Coda.**"

D.C. al Fine
- Go back to the beginning of the song and play until the measure marked "***Fine***" (end).

- Repeat measures between signs.

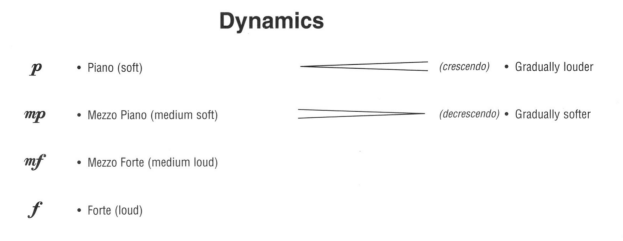

(accent)
- Accentuate the note (play initial attack louder).

(staccato)
- Play the note short.

- When a repeated section has different endings, play the first ending only the first time and the second ending only the second time.

Dynamics

p
- Piano (soft)

mp
- Mezzo Piano (medium soft)

mf
- Mezzo Forte (medium loud)

f
- Forte (loud)

(crescendo)
- Gradually louder

(decrescendo)
- Gradually softer

Across the Universe

Words and Music by John Lennon and Paul McCartney

Verse
Slowly

C · · · · · · · · · Am · · · · · · · · · Em

1. Words are flow-ing out ____ like end-less rain in-to a pa-per cup; they

8va throughout

7↑ 7↑ 7↑ 7↑ 7↓   6↓ 6↑ 6↓   6↑ 6↓ 6↑ 6↓ 6↑ 6↓ 6↑   6↓

Dm7 · · · · · · · · · · · · · · · · · · G7

slith - er while _ they pass, they slip a - way ____ a-cross the un-i - verse. _

5↓ 6↑ 5↓   6↑ 5↓ 6↑ 5↓ 6↑ 6↑   6↓ 6↑ 6↓ 6↑ 6↓ 7↓ 6↓ 7↓

C · · · · · · · · · Am · · · · · · · · · Em

Pools of sor - row, waves of joy are drift - ing through my o - pened mind, _ pos-

7↑ 7↑ 7↑ 7↑ 7↓ 6↓ 6↑ 6↓   6↑ 6↓ 6↑ 6↓ 6↑ 6↓ 6↑   6↓

Dm7 · · · · · · · · · · Fm

sess - ing and ca - ress - ing me. _____

5↓ 6↑   5↓ 6↑   5↓ 5↑ 4↓ 4↑

𝄋 Chorus

C

Jai ____ Gu - ru _____ De - va. ____

6↑ 5↑ 6↑ 7↑   7↓ 8↓ 7↑ 7↑

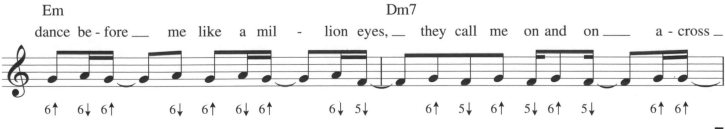

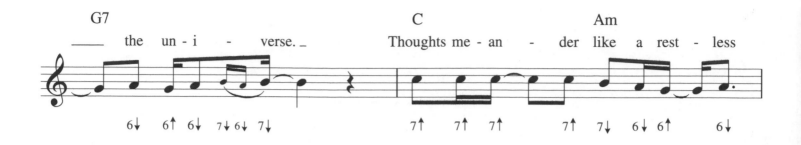

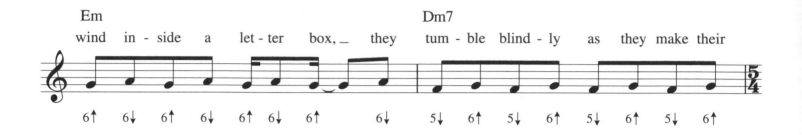

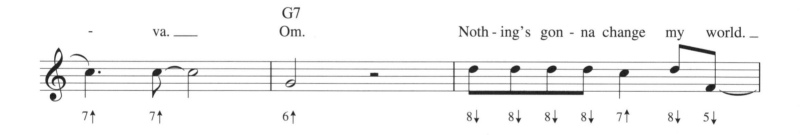

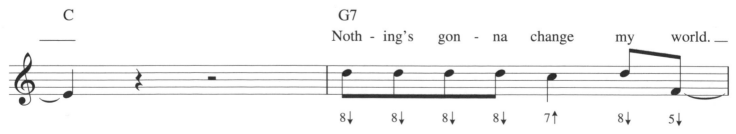

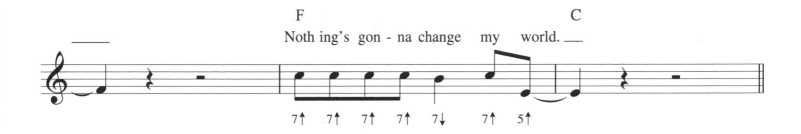

Nothing's gon-na change my world. ___

F   C

7↑ 7↑ 7↑ 7↑ 7↓ 7↑ 5↑

Verse

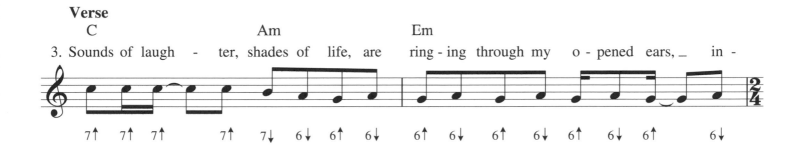

C   Am   Em

3. Sounds of laugh - ter, shades of life, are ring-ing through my o-pened ears, ___ in -

7↑ 7↑ 7↑ 7↑ 7↓ 6↓ 6↑ 6↓ 6↑ 6↓ 6↑ 6↓ 6↑ 6↓ 6↑ 6↓

Dm7   Fm

cit - ing and in - vit - ing me. _____

5↓ 6↑ 5↓ 6↑ 5↓ 5↑ 4↓ 4↑

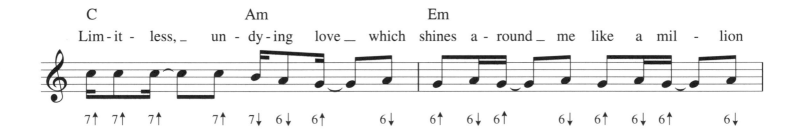

C   Am   Em

Lim - it - less, _ un - dy - ing love _ which shines a - round _ me like a mil - lion

7↑ 7↑ 7↑ 7↑ 7↓ 6↓ 6↑ 6↓ 6↑ 6↓ 6↑ 6↓ 6↑ 6↓ 6↑ 6↓

D.S. al Coda

Dm7   G7

suns, it calls me on and on ___ a - cross the un - i - verse. ___

5↓ 6↑ 5↓ 6↑ 5↓ 6↑ 5↓ 6↑ 6↑ 6↓ 6↑ 6↓ 7↓ 6↓ 7↓

⊕ Coda

Play 6 times & fade

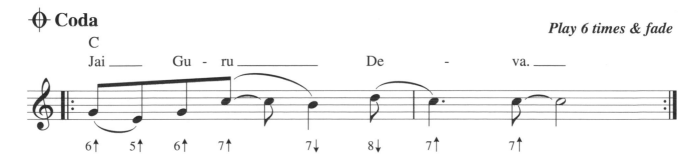

C

Jai ___ Gu - ru _____ De - va. ___

6↑ 5↑ 6↑ 7↑ 7↓ 8↓ 7↑ 7↑

9

And I Love Her

Words and Music by John Lennon and Paul McCartney

Because

Words and Music by John Lennon and Paul McCartney

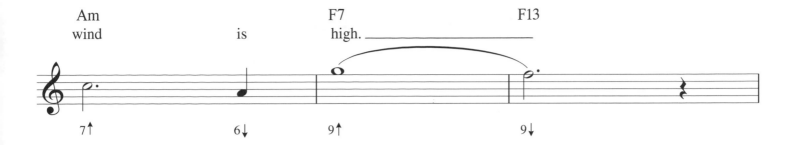

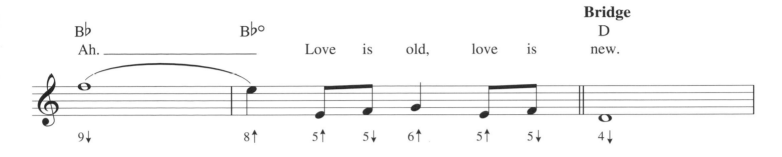

Bridge

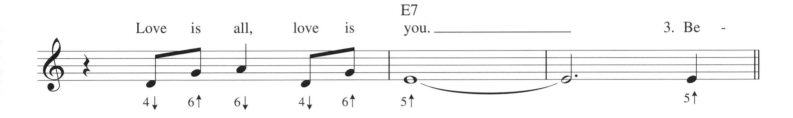

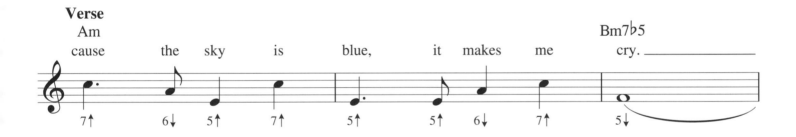

Verse

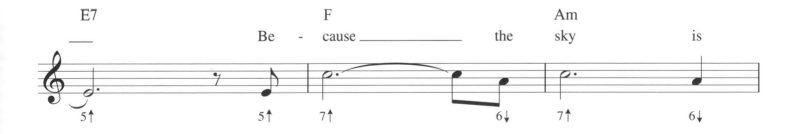

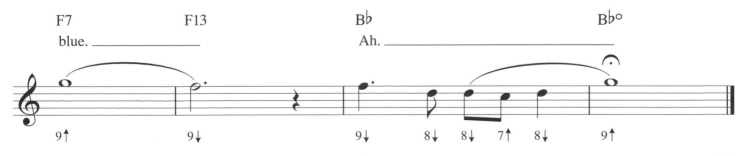

All My Loving

Words and Music by John Lennon and Paul McCartney

Verse

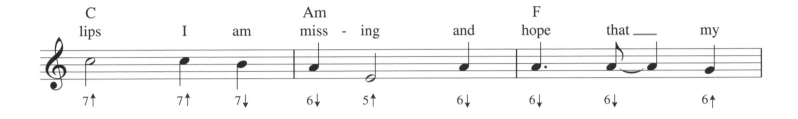

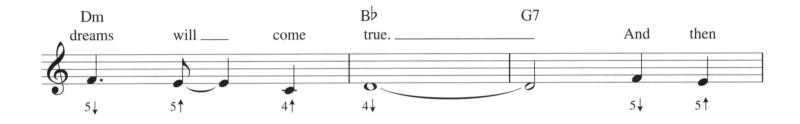

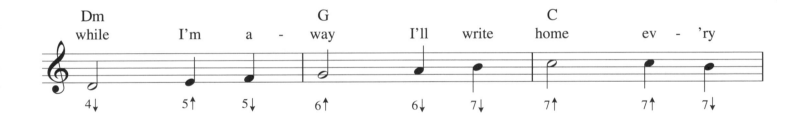

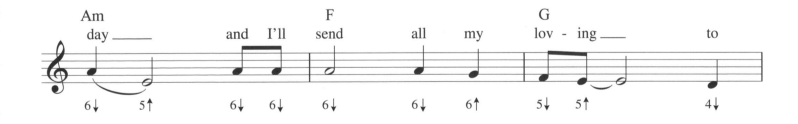

Chorus

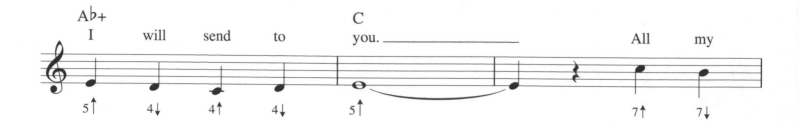

D.S. al Coda

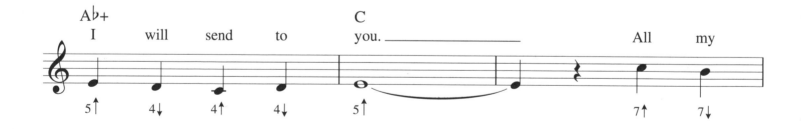

Don't Let Me Down

Words and Music by John Lennon and Paul McCartney

Dm
down. _____

Don't let me

8↓ 7↑ 6↓ 5↑ 5↓ 5↑ 5↓ 5↑ 5↓ 5↑ 5↓ 5↓   8↑ 8↑ 8↑
         4 4 4 4   4 4 4   4 4
                                          3

C
down. _____

I'm in love for the

7↑ 6↓ 6↑   4↓ 4↓ 5↑ 2↓ 2↑ 3↑   6↑ 5↑ 6↑ 6↑ 5↑
           3 3 4 1 1 2
                          1

Bridge
C
first time.

Don't cha know __ it's gon - na last? __

6↑ 6↑   6↑ 6↓ 7↑   6↓ 6↑ 5↑ 6↑

G7
_____

It's a love __ that lasts __ for - ev - er.

6↑ 6↑ 9↓   9↓ 8↑   8↓ 8↓   8↓

C

It's a love __ that had __ no _____ past. _____

6↑ 6↑ 9↓   9↓ 8↑   8↓ 8↑ 8↓ 7↑ 6↑

⊕ **Coda**

D.S. al Coda

C

Don't let me   down.

8↑ 8↓ 8↓   7↑   7 7↑ 6 6↑ 4 5↓ 5↑
                    6 6 5 5   3 4   4
                    5 5 4 4   2 3 3
                                     2

Eight Days a Week

Words and Music by John Lennon and Paul McCartney

Bridge

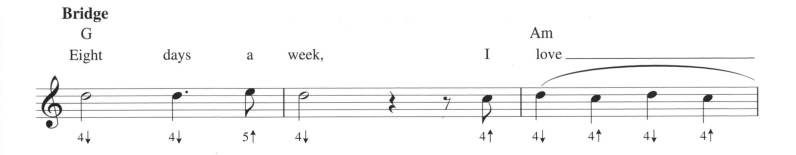

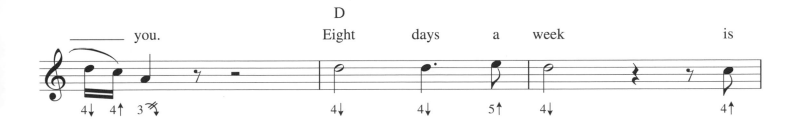

D.S. al Coda
(take repeat)

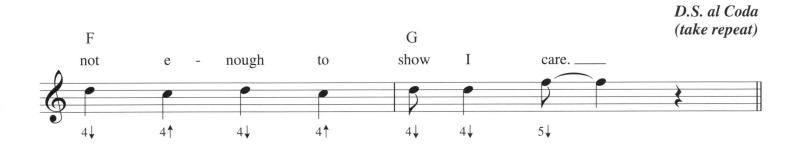

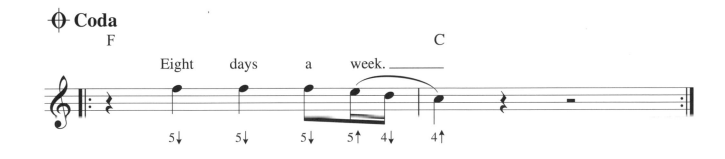

Outro

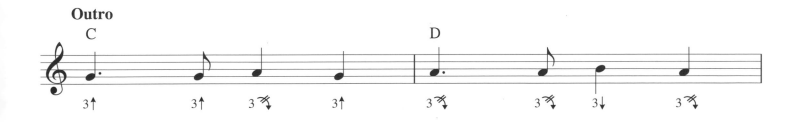

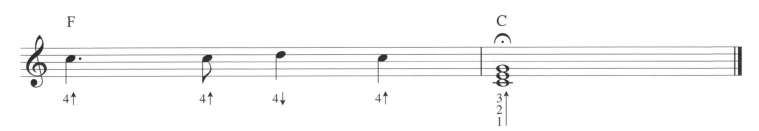

Golden Slumbers

Words and Music by John Lennon and Paul McCartney

Chorus

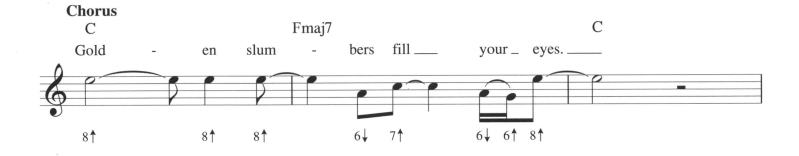

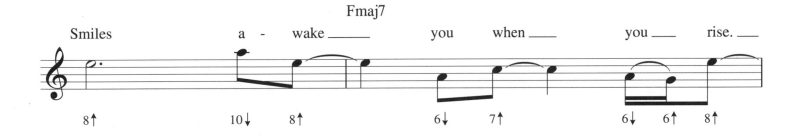

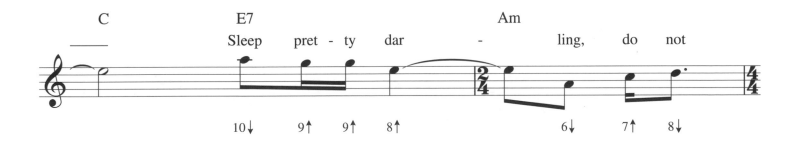

D.C. al Fine

Hello, Goodbye

Words and Music by John Lennon and Paul McCartney

Verse
Moderately

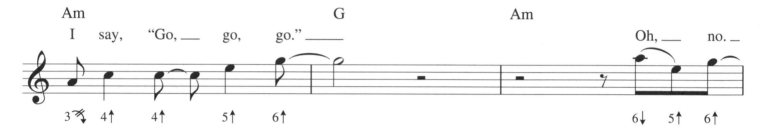

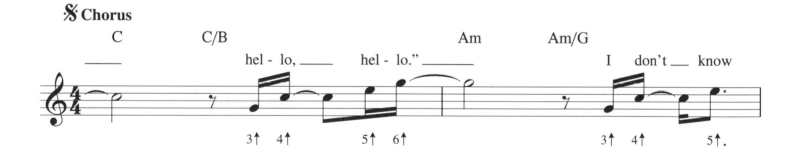

𝄋 Chorus

Am   Am/G   F   B♭9   C

I don't __ know why you say, "Good - bye." __ I say, "Hel - lo." ___

3↑ 4↑   5↑   5↓ 5↓ 5↑ 4↓ 4↑   4↑ 4↑ 3↗ 4↑

Verse

F6   C   G

2. I say, "High." __   You say, "Low." __   You say, "Why." __   And

4↓ 5↓ 5↓   4↑ 5↑ 5↑   3↓ 4↓ 4↓   3↑

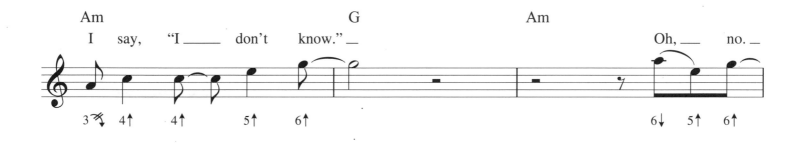

Am   G   Am

I say, "I ____ don't know." __   Oh, __ no. __

3↗ 4↑ 4↑ 5↑ 6↑   6↓ 5↑ 6↑

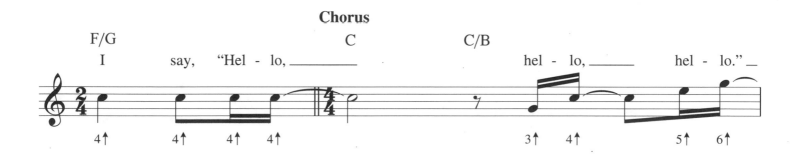

G

You   say, "Good - bye." __   And

6↑   5↑ 4↑ 4↓   3↑

Chorus

F/G   C   C/B

I   say, "Hel - lo, _____   hel - lo, _____   hel - lo." __

4↑   4↑ 4↑ 4↑   3↑ 4↑   5↑ 6↑

Am   Am/G   F   Fm/A♭

I don't __ know   why you say, "Good - bye." __   I say, "Hel - lo, __

3↑ 4↑   5↑   5↓ 5↓ 5↑ 4↓ 4↑   4↑ 4↑ 3↗ 4↑

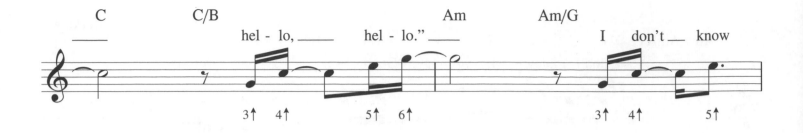

Interlude

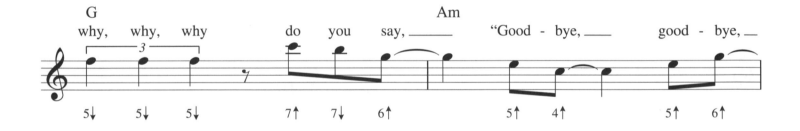

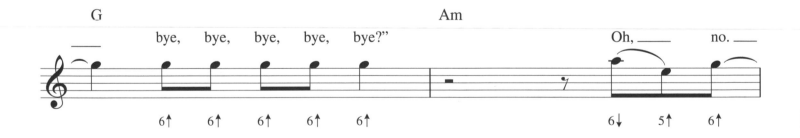

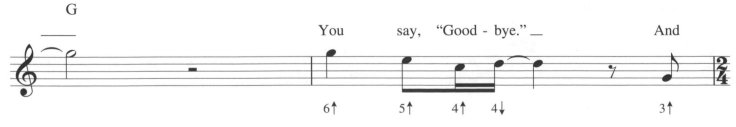

26

Coda

D.S. al Coda

Verse

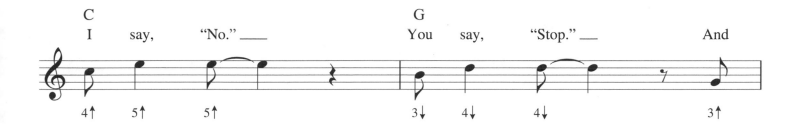

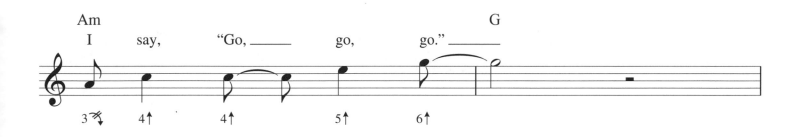

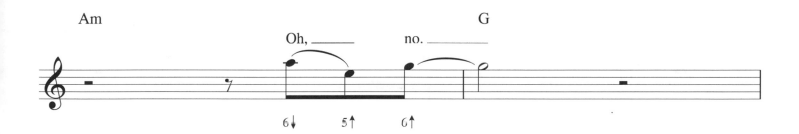

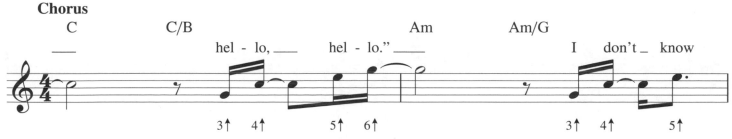

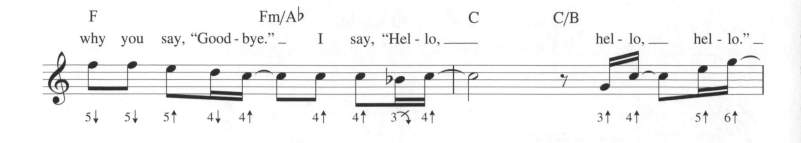

F   Fm/A♭   C   C/B

why you say, "Good - bye." _ I say, "Hel - lo, _____ hel - lo, _____ hel - lo." _

5↓ 5↓ 5↑ 4↓ 4↑ 4↑ 4↑ 3↘ 4↑   3↑ 4↑ 5↑ 6↑

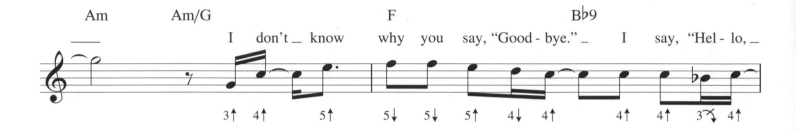

Am   Am/G   F   B♭9

_ I don't _ know why you say, "Good - bye." _ I say, "Hel - lo, _

3↑ 4↑ 5↑ 5↓ 5↓ 5↑ 4↓ 4↑ 4↑ 4↑ 3↘ 4↑

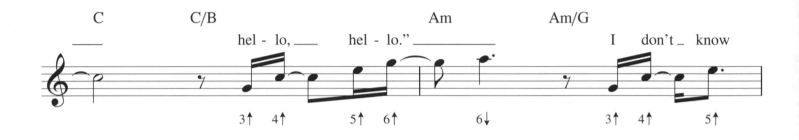

C   C/B   Am   Am/G

_ hel - lo, _____ hel - lo." _____ I don't _ know

3↑ 4↑ 5↑ 6↑ 6↓   3↑ 4↑ 5↑

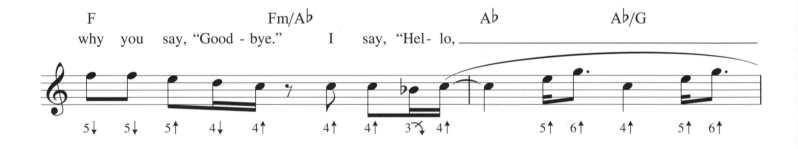

F   Fm/A♭   A♭   A♭/G

why you say, "Good - bye." I say, "Hel - lo, _____

5↓ 5↓ 5↑ 4↓ 4↑ 4↑ 4↑ 3↘ 4↑   5↑ 6↑ 4↑ 5↑ 6↑

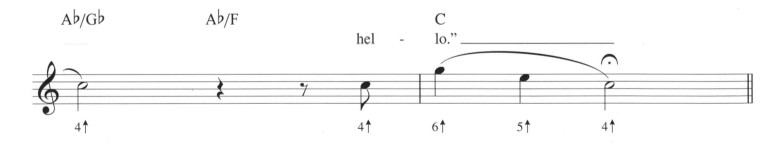

A♭/G♭   A♭/F   C

hel - lo." _____

4↑   4↑ 6↑ 5↑ 4↑

Outro   *Play 8 times & fade*

C

Hey - la,   he - ba, hel - lo - a.

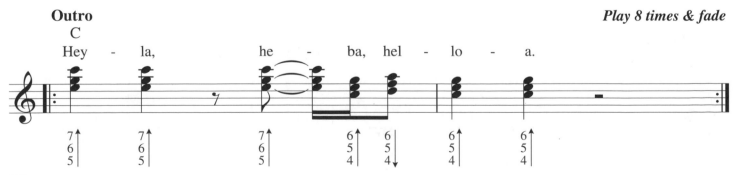

7↑ 7↑ 7↑ 6↑ 6 6↑ 6↑
6 6 6 5 5 5 5
5 5 5 4 4↓ 4 4

Here Comes the Sun

Words and Music by George Harrison

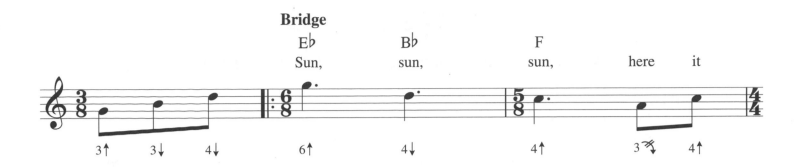

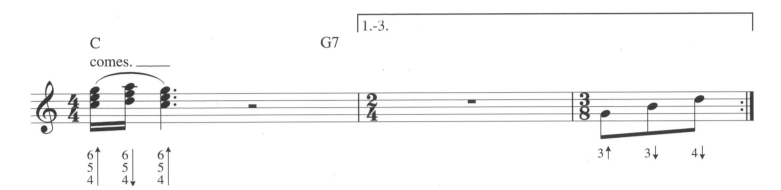

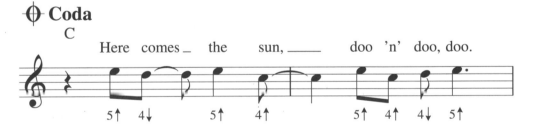

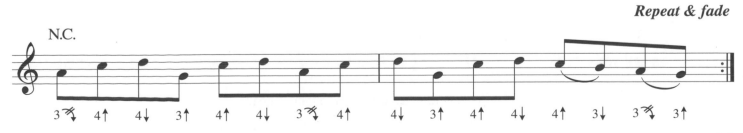

Help!

Words and Music by John Lennon and Paul McCartney

I Want to Hold Your Hand

Words and Music by John Lennon and Paul McCartney

Ob-La-Di, Ob-La-Da

Words and Music by John Lennon and Paul McCartney

I Will

Words and Music by John Lennon and Paul McCartney

If I Fell

Words and Music by John Lennon and Paul McCartney

*Tied on repeat.

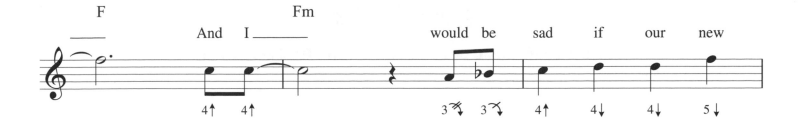

F   Fm

And I ———   would be sad if our new

C   G7   **Verse** C   Dm

love was in vain.   3., 4. So I hope you

Em   Dm   G7

see that I would love to love you

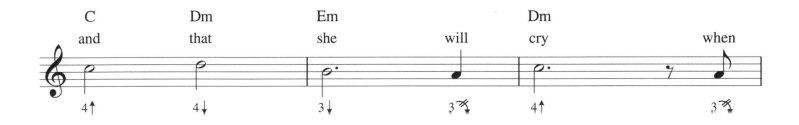

C   Dm   Em   Dm

and that she will cry when

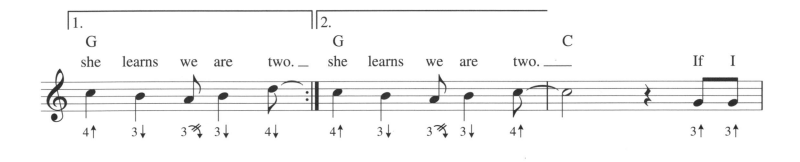

1.   2.

G   G   C

she learns we are two.— she learns we are two.——— If I

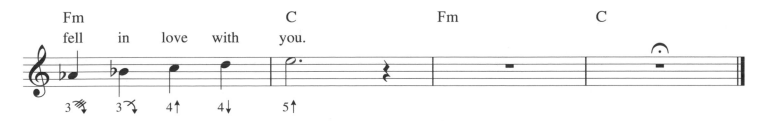

Fm   C   Fm   C

fell in love with you.

Let It Be

Words and Music by John Lennon and Paul McCartney

Chorus

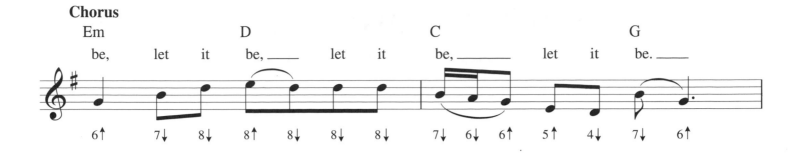

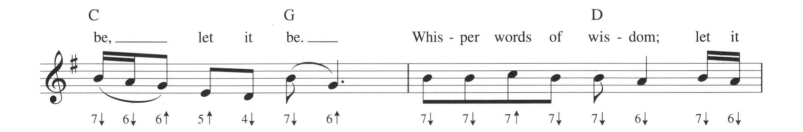

Outro

Mother Nature's Son

Words and Music by John Lennon and Paul McCartney

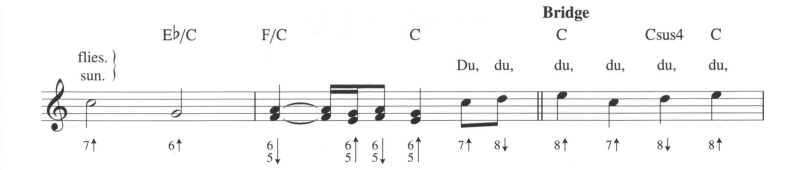

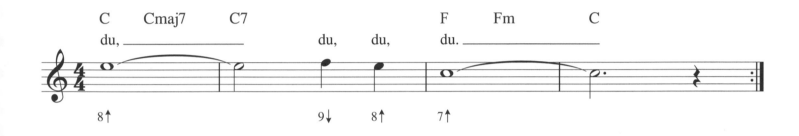

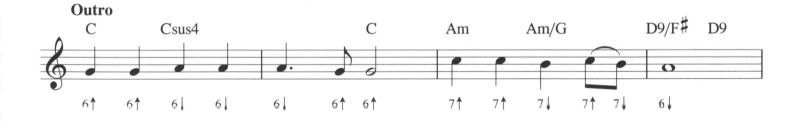

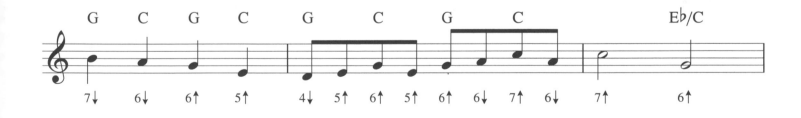

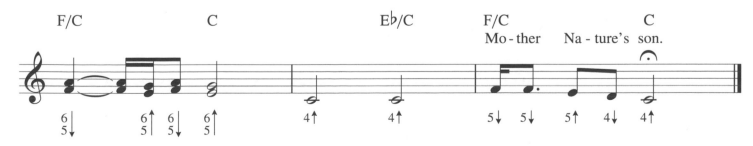

Nowhere Man

Words and Music by John Lennon and Paul McCartney

Verse
Moderately

1. He's a real no-where man, sit-ting in ___ his no-where land,

mak-ing all ___ his no-where plans for no - bod-y. _____

Verse

2. Does-n't have ___ a point of view, ___ knows not where he's go-ing to. ___

Is-n't he ___ a bit like you and me? _____ No - where

Bridge

man, please lis-ten. You don't know what you're miss-ing. No-where

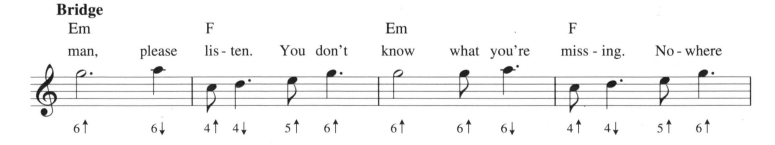

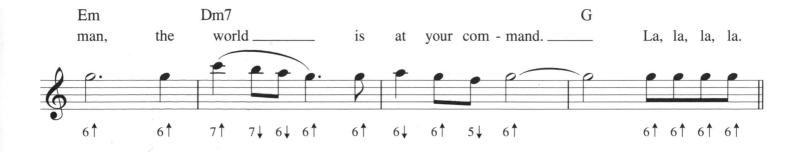

Em   Dm7   G

man,   the   world _____ is   at   your   com - mand. _____   La, la, la, la.

6↑   6↑   7↑ 7↓ 6↓ 6↑   6↑   6↓   6↑   5↓ 6↑   6↑ 6↑ 6↑ 6↑

Interlude

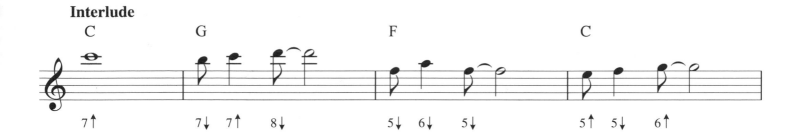

C   G   F   C

7↑   7↓ 7↑   8↓   5↓ 6↓   5↓   5↑ 5↓   6↑

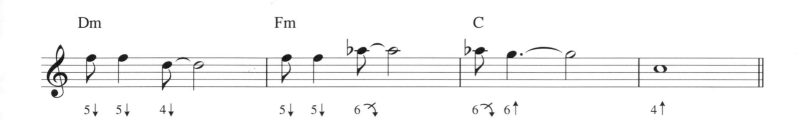

Dm   Fm   C

5↓ 5↓ 4↓   5↓ 5↓   6↘   6↘ 6↑   4↑

Verse

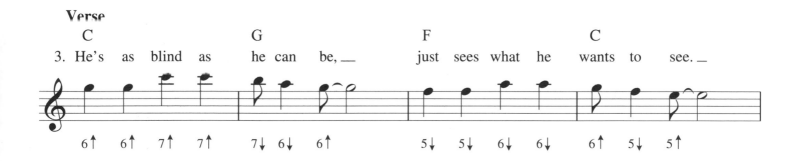

C   G   F   C

3. He's   as   blind   as   he can   be, __   just   sees   what   he   wants   to   see. __

6↑ 6↑ 7↑ 7↑   7↓ 6↓ 6↑   5↓ 5↓ 6↓ 6↓   6↑ 5↓ 5↑

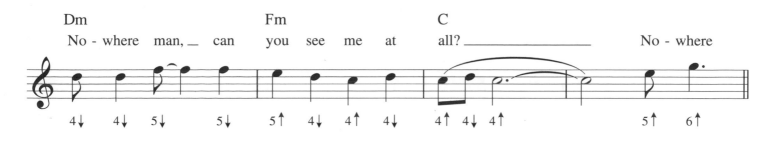

Dm   Fm   C

No - where man, __ can   you   see   me   at   all? _____   No - where

4↓   4↓   5↓   5↓   5↑ 4↓ 4↑ 4↓   4↑ 4↓ 4↑   5↑   6↑

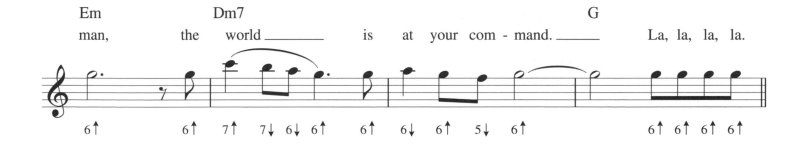

man, the world _____ is at your com - mand. _____ La, la, la, la.

Verse

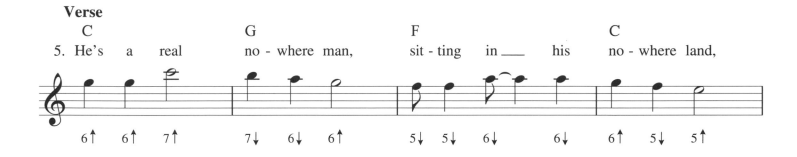

5. He's a real no - where man, sit - ting in _____ his no - where land,

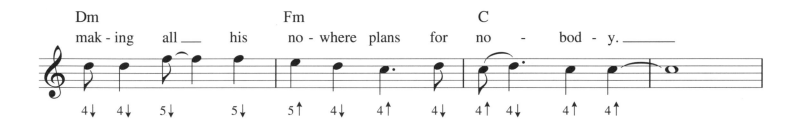

mak - ing all _____ his no - where plans for no - bod - y. _____

Mak - ing all _____ his no - where plans for no - bod - y. _____

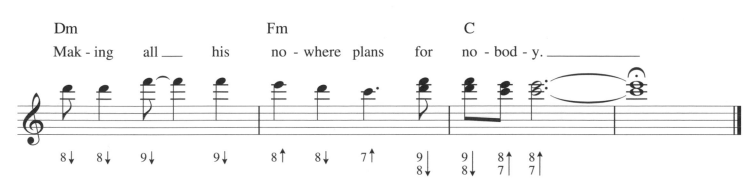

Mak - ing all _____ his no - where plans for no - bod - y. _____

Paperback Writer

Words and Music by John Lennon and Paul McCartney

With a Little Help from My Friends

Words and Music by John Lennon and Paul McCartney

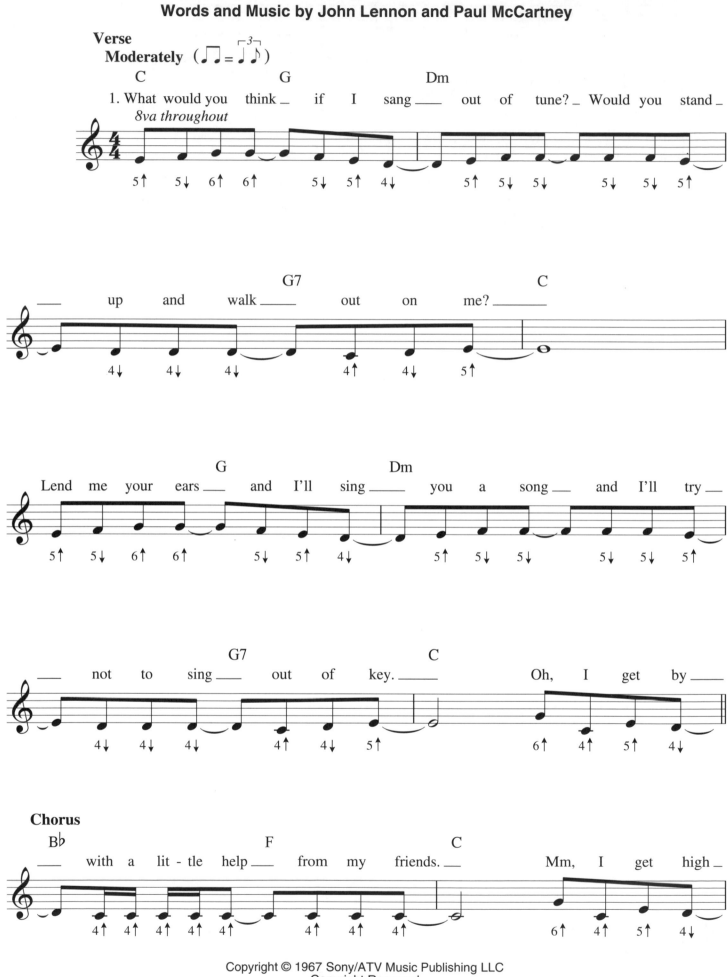

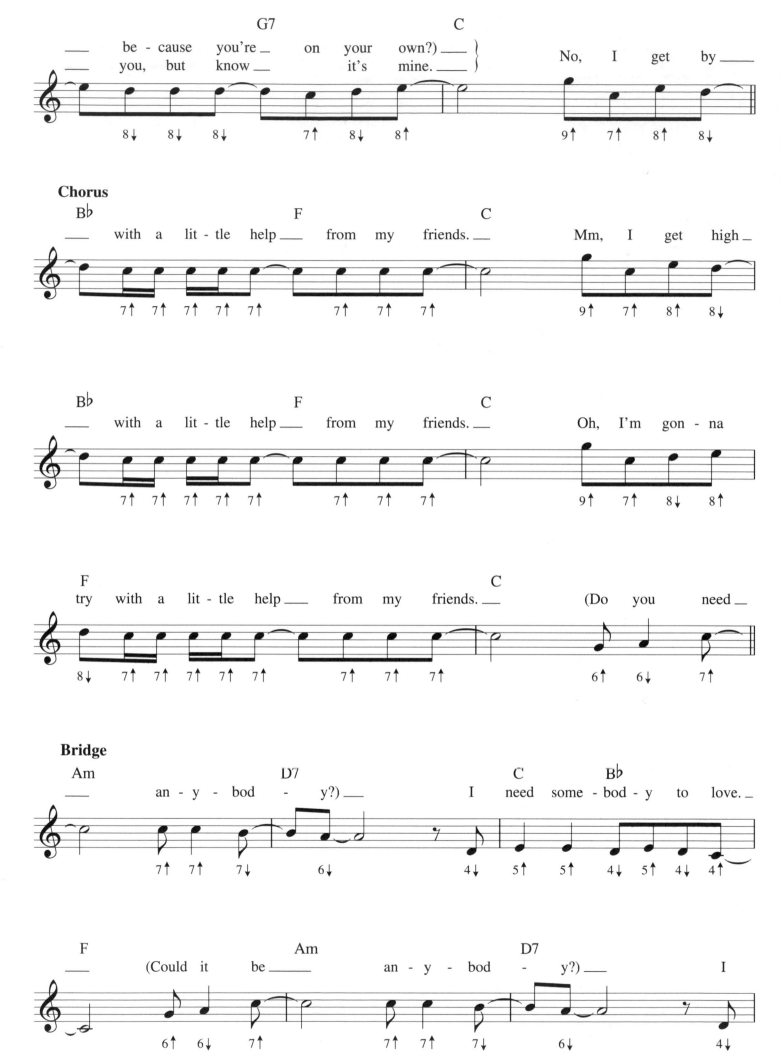

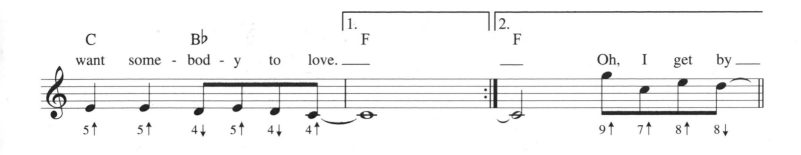

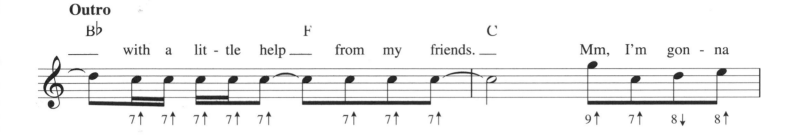

Outro

Yellow Submarine

Words and Music by John Lennon and Paul McCartney

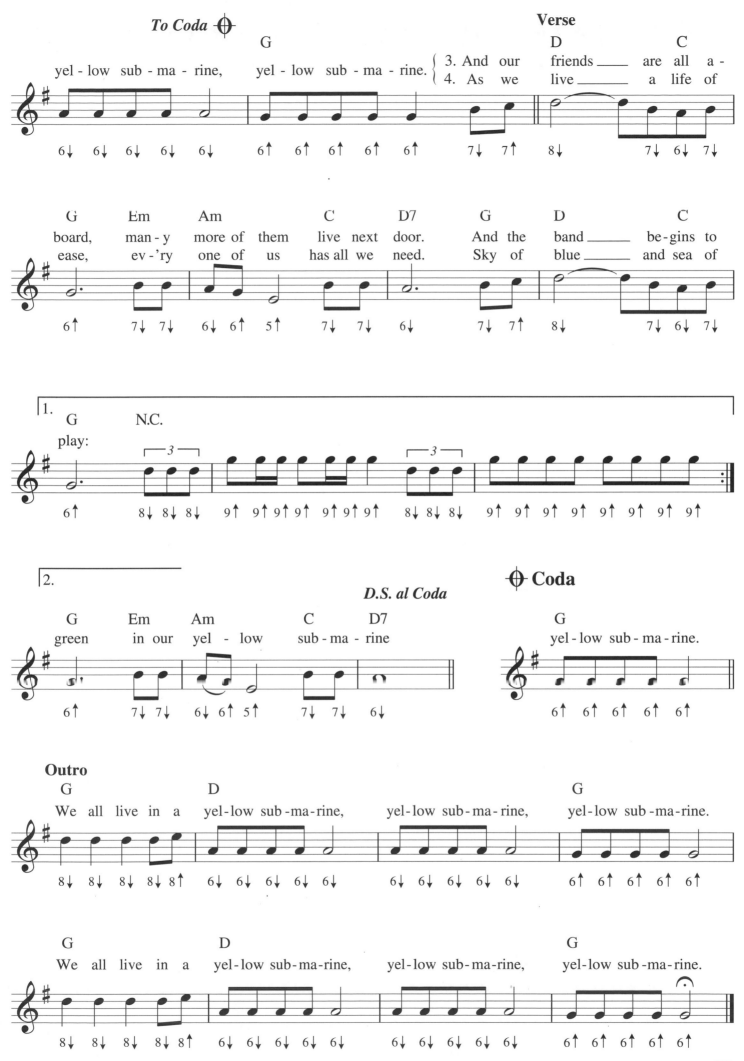

You've Got to Hide Your Love Away

Words and Music by John Lennon and Paul McCartney

We Can Work It Out

Words and Music by John Lennon and Paul McCartney

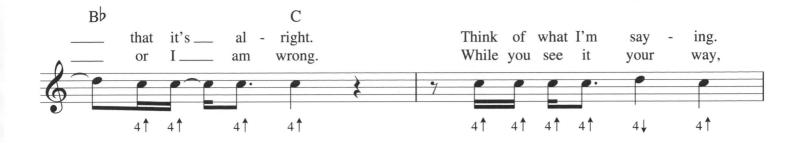

Bb

that it's ___ al - right.
or I ___ am wrong.

C

Think of what I'm say - ing.
While you see it your way,

4↑ 4↑ 4↑ 4↑   4↑ 4↑ 4↑ 4↑ 4↓ 4↑

To Coda ⊕

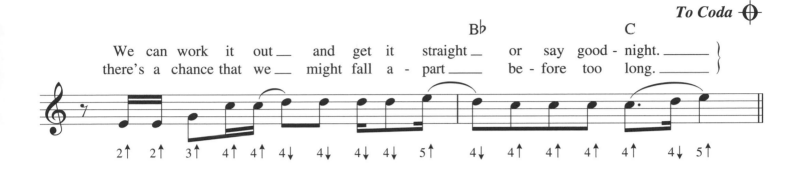

We can work it out ___ and get it straight ___ or say good - night. ___
there's a chance that we ___ might fall a - part ___ be - fore too long. ___

Bb   C

2↑ 2↑ 3↑ 4↑ 4↑ 4↓ 4↓ 4↓ 4↓ 5↑   4↓ 4↑ 4↑ 4↑ 4↑ 4↓ 5↑

Chorus

F   C   F   G

We can work it out. ___   We can work it out. ___

6↑ 5↓ 5↓ 4↑ 4↑   6↑ 5↓ 5↓ 4↑ 4↑ 3↓

Bridge

Am   Am/G

Life is ver - y short ___ and there's no time ___

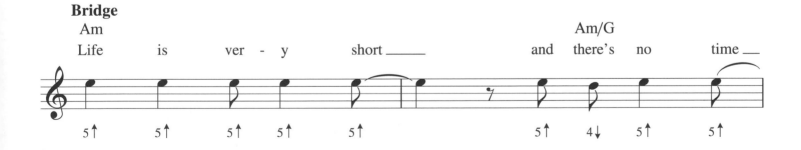

5↑ 5↑ 5↑ 5↑ 5↑   5↑ 4↓ 5↑ 5↑

F   E

___ for fuss - ing and

3
5↓ 5↑ 4↓ 4↑ 3↓   3↓ 5↑ 5↑ 5↑

63